JE PAR
Parker, Victoria.
Blue with other colors

11/10 - 20

Mixing Colors

Blue

with Other Colors

Victoria Parker

Raintree

Chicago, Illinois

Printed and bound in China.
08 07 06 05 04
10 9 8 7 6 5 4 3 2 1

Library of Congress Cataloging-in-Publication Data:
Parker, Victoria.
  Blue with other colors / Victoria Parker.
     p. cm. -- (Mixing colors)
Summary: Shows different shades of blue and the colors that result when
blue is mixed with other colors.
Includes bibliographical references and index.
  ISBN 1-4109-0751-1 (lib. bdg. : hardcover) -- ISBN 1-4109-0756-2
(pbk.)
  1. Blue--Juvenile literature. 2. Colors--Juvenile literature. [1.
Blue. 2. Color.] I. Title. II. Series: Parker, Victoria. Mixing
colors.
  QC495.5.P375 2004
  535.6--dc22
                         2003019140

Acknowledgments
The publishers would like to thank the following for permission to reproduce photographs:
pp. 4, 5, 6, 7, 8, 9, 10, 11, 12, 13, 14, 15, 16, 17, 18, 19, 20, 21 Trevor Clifford; p. 22 Corbis;
p. 23 Jill Birschbach/Heinemann Library

Cover photograph reproduced with permission of Trevor Clifford

Every effort has been made to contact copyright holders of any material reproduced in this book.
Any omissions will be rectified in subsequent printings if notice is given to the publishers.

Some words are shown in bold, **like this.** You can find out
what they mean by looking in the glossary on page 24.

Contents

The Color Blue

Blue is a **primary color**.

You can mix it with other colors.

What Is Blue?

Can you think of some things that are blue?

blue beads

blue toy car

blue gloves

Shades of Blue

Some blues are dark.
Other blues are light.

cyan

sapphire

azure

royal

midnight

Each different blue is called a **shade**.

Blue and Red

Mix red and blue paint.

Red and blue
make purple.

Indigo

Mix a little red with some blue paint.

You get a **shade** of dark blue called indigo.

13

Violet

Mix a lot of red with some blue paint.

You get a shade called **violet.**

15

Blue and Yellow

Paint some blue dots.

Paint some yellow dots.

Blue and yellow make green!

17

Blue and Green

Color with a blue crayon.

Color with a green crayon.

Blue and green make turquoise.

peacock

Peacock feathers are turquoise.

Blue and Black

Mix some black paint with blue.

You get midnight blue, like the sky at night.

A Blue and White Treat

Mix some blueberries
with some white ice cream.

You get a blue milkshake.

Glossary

midnight the last hour of the day

peacock bird with a large tail turquoise feathers

primary color color that cannot be made by mixing together other colors

shade a color that is lighter or darker. Dark blue, light blue, and turquoise look different, but they are all shades of blue.

Index

24